FIREFIGHTER, FIREFIGHTER, WHO DO YOU SEE?

By Anthony Segura

Illustrated by Ros Webb

To all the children out there. Dream big.
Be who you want to be. Be The Change.

Hi Mama! Hi Pops! Hi Baby Sister! Hi Edlin!
Hi Ollie!

Waves

To everyone who has supported my
endeavors and continues to believe in me!

Ana Lopez Negrete

Yecenia Munoz

Bri Rivera

Cody Moran

Jason Merino

Mayra Paz

Sebastian Estrada

Matt Lantrip

Karla Vasquez

Elisa Palomo

Elizabeth Gutierrez

Alejandra Godinez

Sisian Grigorian

Mama

Jo Anna Sanchez

Edlin Gutierrez ♥

Aaron Martinez

Sister

Tara Harcourt

Jay Udeshi

Pops

Kira Reed

Diana Chevez

Wendy Paniagua

Trey Seal

Roxy Peralta

Violette Fierro

Laith Al-Badawi

Leah Mashian

Claudia Sneed

Firefighter, Firefighter,
Who do you see?

I see a Police Officer
in our community.

Police Officer,
Police Officer,
Who do you see?
POLICE

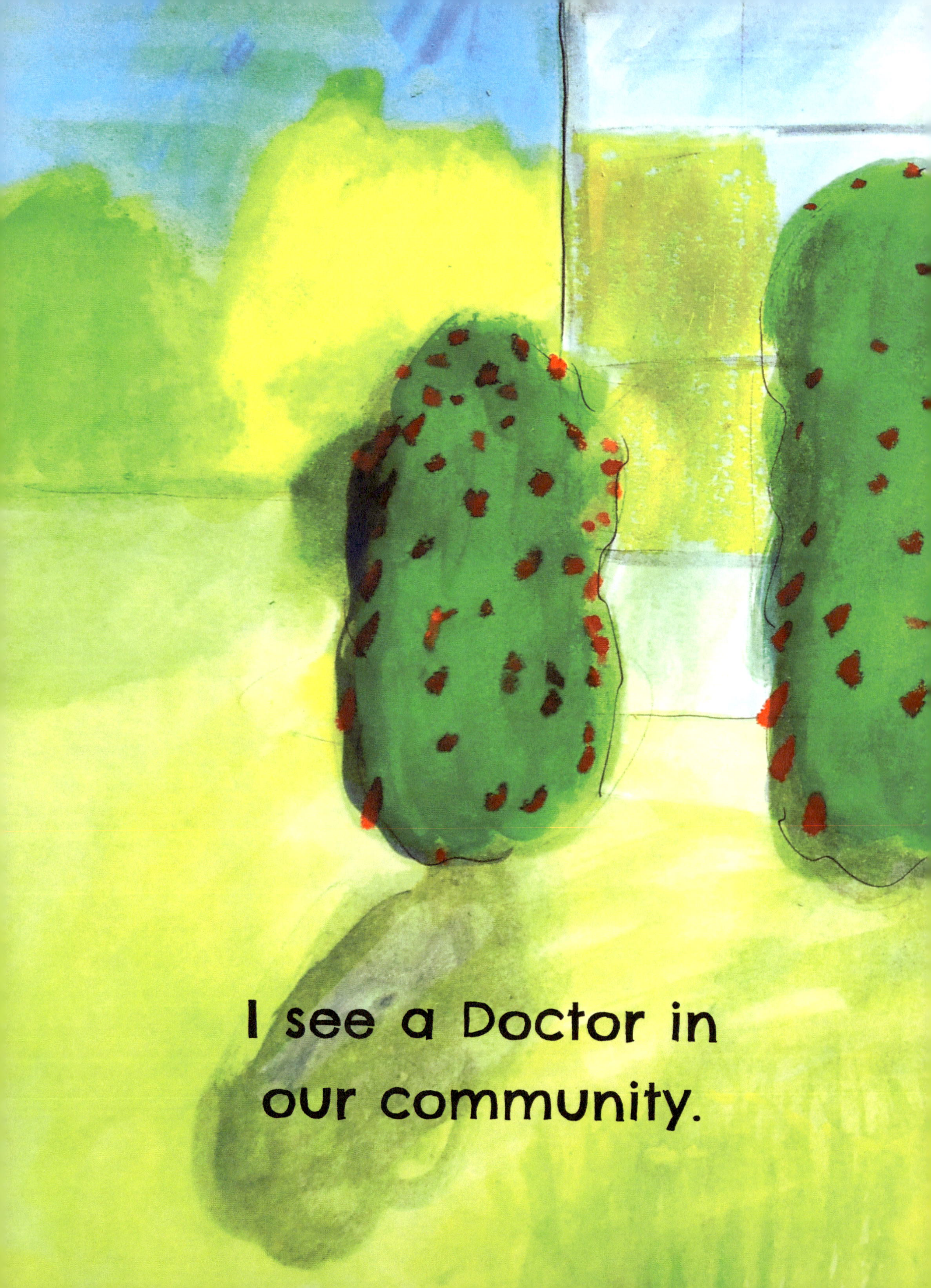
I see a Doctor in
our community.

Doctor, Doctor,
Who do you see?
HOSPITAL

I see a Teacher in our community.

Teacher, Teacher, Who do you see?

I see an Athlete in our community.

Athlete, Athlete,
Who do you see?

I see a Farmer in our community.

Farmer, Farmer,
Who do you see?

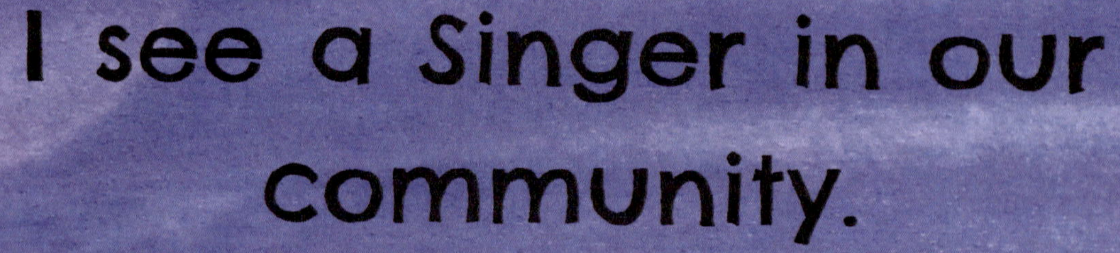

I see a Singer in our
community.

Singer, Singer,
Who do you see?

I see a Construction
Worker in our
community.

Construction Worker,
Construction Worker,
Who do you see?

I see a Chef in
our community.

Chef, Chef,
Who do you see?

I see workers in our community.

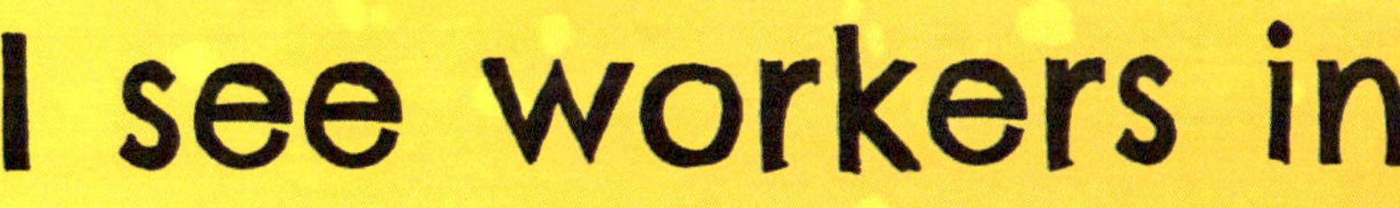

Dear Future Self,

I want to be a _______________
when I grow up.

Draw a picture below